100 QUESTIONS AND ANSWERS

EXPL🧭RERS
AND VOYAGES OF DISCOVERY

Written by
Margarette Lincoln

Edited by
Nicola Wright & Dee Turner

Designed by
David Anstey

Illustrated by
Mainline Design, Richard Draper & Peter Bull

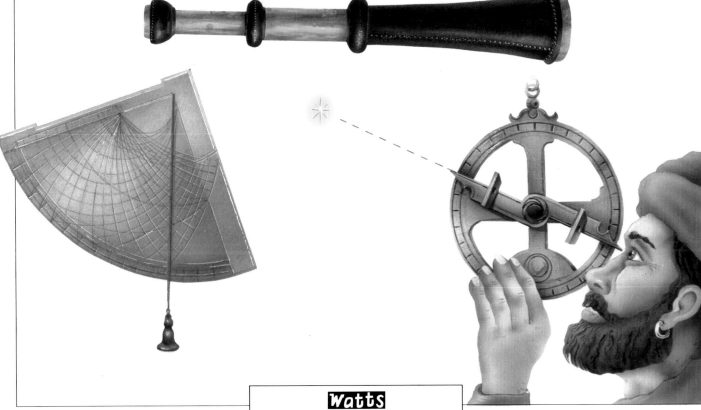

watts
LONDON • NEW YORK • SYDNEY

Dr Margarette Lincoln is Assistant Head of Education at the National Maritime Museum, London. She has taught in schools and universities. Her publications include resource materials for teachers and several children's books.

This book was created by Zigzag Publishing Ltd, 5 High Street, Cuckfield, Sussex RH17 5EN, England

Series concept: Tony Potter
Design Manager: Kate Buxton
Production: Zoë Fawcett

Colour separations: RCS Graphics Ltd, Leeds
Printed in Belgium

First published in 1993 by Watts Books

BRITISH LIBRARY CATALOGUING IN PUBLICATION DATA
A catalogue record for this book is available from the British Library.

Dewey Decimal Classification 910.9

UK ISBN 0 7496 1333 5
10 9 8 7 6 5 4 3 2 1

Contents

About this book

This book answers all your questions about people's exploration of the world from the earliest recorded times to the present day. It is packed full of fascinating facts about heroic journeys across unknown oceans, through hostile lands, into space and under the sea.

What were the earliest boats made from? Who first sailed around the world? Which explorers first saw kangaroos? What is a diving bell? What do astronauts eat? These are just some of the many questions you will find out the answers to.

Who were the first explorers?

Phoenicians ruled the Mediterranean for 1000 years from 1400 BC.

The earliest explorers lived in pre-historic times, more than half a million years ago. They were Stone Age people in the land now called Africa, searching for new sources of food and shelter.

Q Why did people begin to explore?

A Exploration was often a question of survival. People hoped to find fresh supplies of food and living materials and often a safer place away from enemies.

Q What were the earliest boats made from?

A Boats might have been made from hollowed-out logs, reeds, or skins stretched over a wooden frame.

Q How did people first explore?

A The first explorers probably travelled on foot or on horseback. But it was easier to travel greater distances across the sea or along rivers by boat.

Q Who were the greatest early explorers to cross oceans?

A The Phoenicians, who lived in what is now Israel, built a large fleet of ships around 800 BC. They travelled as far as Africa and the British Isles to trade.

Q What cargoes did ships carry?

A Egyptian ships carried wood, ivory, silver, gold, cloth and spices. They also carried animals.

Q Who first sailed around Africa?

A The dangerous journey round what is now called the Cape of Good Hope was made by the Phoenicians in about 600 BC .

In about 1500 BC, Queen Hatshepsut of Egypt sent five ships to Punt (now called Somalia) for spices, monkeys, dogs and minerals.

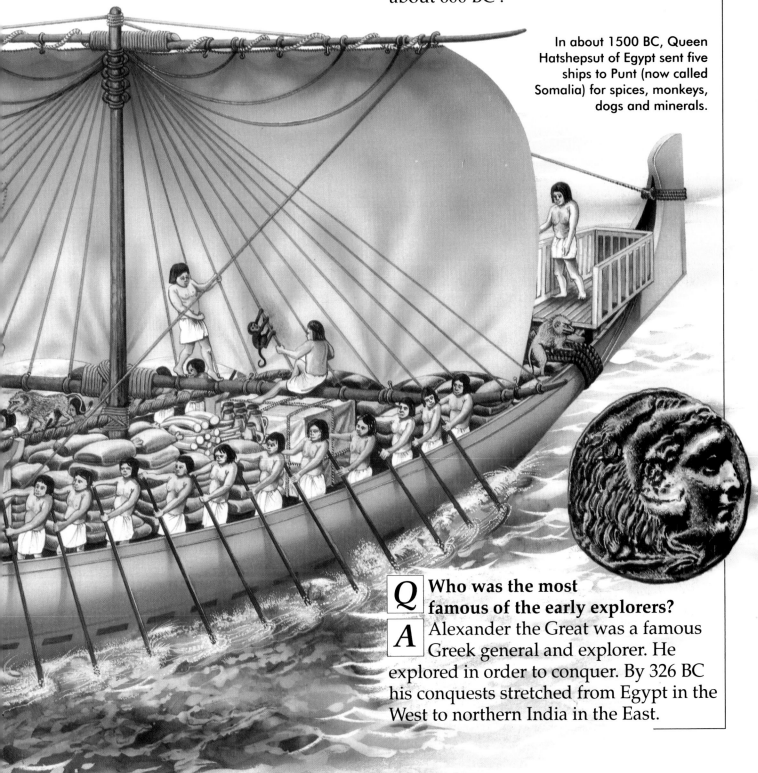

Q Who was the most famous of the early explorers?

A Alexander the Great was a famous Greek general and explorer. He explored in order to conquer. By 326 BC his conquests stretched from Egypt in the West to northern India in the East.

Viking sailors sometimes relied on the instinct of birds. From time to time they would release a raven and follow it, hoping it would lead them to land.

Before modern instruments such as radar and radio were invented, explorers had to use other methods to discover their position at sea and in strange lands.

About 3000 years ago, Polynesians were exploring the Pacific islands in canoes. To navigate they studied the positions of the stars, wind direction and the pattern of ocean waves.

Q How did the earliest explorers navigate?

A Navigators studied the position of the Moon, Sun and stars. Some also knew how to sail along a given latitude (distance north or south of a line called the Equator which runs round the middle of the Earth).

Q How did explorers find remote islands?

A Early sailors could guess where land lay from the behaviour of sea creatures and from the shape and size of waves. Their boats may have been carried across the ocean by currents.

Q How did sailors know they were near land if they didn't have a chart?

A Sailors knew they were near land when they saw birds or floating vegetation. Sometimes the colour of the sea or the shape of clouds changed near land.

The telescope was
invented in the
early 17th century.

The telescope was
invented in the
early 17th century.

Q Who invented the compass?

A The Chinese invented the first compass about 4000 years ago. However, European explorers did not use them until about 1000 years ago.

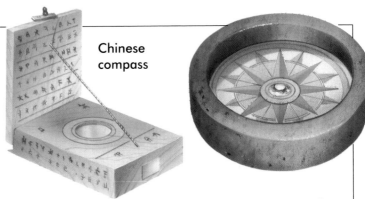

Chinese compass

A compass consists of a magnetized needle on a pivot. Because of the Earth's magnetism, the needle always points to magnetic north.

Early charts, called portulan charts, were drawn on stretched animal skin (parchment).

Q What were early charts like?

A In the 15th century, charts showed coastal features, ports and danger spots. Direction lines radiated out from compass points to help seamen follow a direct course from one place to another.

Q What was a quadrant used for?

A The quadrant was the earliest instrument used to measure the height of the Sun or stars. It was invented by the Arabs. In the 15th century, seamen used it to work out their latitude.

The sights of a quadrant were lined up with the Sun or a star. The plumb line showed the number of degrees above the horizon to work out a ship's position at sea.

Q What was an astrolabe?

A Like the quadrant, the astrolabe was used to work out latitude. Both instruments were fairly inaccurate at sea, when readings were taken on a rolling deck.

Astrolabes were made of brass. There were two holes at either end of the arm, which were lined up so the Sun or a star shone through. The arm then showed the height above the horizon.

Some Vikings dared to sail into the unknown Atlantic - to the Faroes, Iceland, Greenland and even America.

How far did the Vikings travel?

Longships were shallow in depth, so Vikings could sail a long way up rivers and estuaries.

The Viking Age began around AD 800 and lasted about 300 years. Vikings explored many distant lands including parts of Russia and North America.

Q Why did the Vikings search for new lands?

A Scandinavia, where the Vikings came from, has long, cold winters and much of the land is difficult to farm. Large families could not grow enough food, so new places to live had to be found.

Q Which was the first Viking colony?

A The Vikings first discovered Iceland in AD 860 when a group of explorers were blown off course. Irish monks had already reached the island about 65 years earlier.

Q What were Viking ships like?

A Vikings warships were known as longships. These were fast, sleek ships, well suited to raiding and long-distance travel.

Astronauts talk to each other by radio as in space there are no air waves to carry sound.

The first person to walk on the Moon was American astronaut Neil Armstrong on 20 July 1969.

Astronauts have to strap themselves into chairs because there is no gravity in a spacecraft and they would float around inside.

Q **How are astronauts able to leave a spacecraft?**

A To travel outside their spacecraft, astronauts wear special sealed suits equipped with oxygen. They may also be linked to the spaceship by a lifeline. A jet booster pack helps them move around.

Q **What do astronauts eat?**

A Food on board a spacecraft is mostly dried then rehydrated before eating. It can be eaten with a spoon and fork or sucked through a tube.

Q **What are space probes?**

A They are unmanned robot spacecraft that explore deep into space for years and transmit information back to Earth. A probe cannot usually return to Earth.

Astronauts do not use a normal toilet. Waste is sucked into bags for disposal back on Earth.

Index

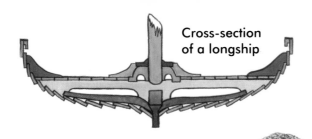

Cross-section of a longship

Q What goods did the Viking traders want?

A They wanted gold, silver, spices, silk, jewellery and iron.

Q Where did the Vikings go?

A The Vikings raided France, Britain and Ireland. They sailed around Spain and into the Mediterranean. Vikings journeyed down the great rivers of Russia to reach the Caspian Sea and the Black Sea. They also crossed the Atlantic to North America.

Q Where did the crew sleep?

A There were no cabins on Viking ships. Viking sailors just covered themselves with animal hides or blankets, though some ships had awnings (roof-coverings). Voyages were not normally made in the coldest winter months .

Q Where did Vikings put their cargo?

A Viking ships did not have decks. Cargo was stored on the floor in the middle of the ship between the oarsmen who sat in the bow and stern.

Knarrs were probably no more than 18m long.

On voyages Vikings ate smoked fish, dried meat and vegetables.

Q What were Viking cargo ships like?

A Vikings carried cargo in ships called knarrs, which were wider than longships and mostly used for coastal trading.

Arab merchants who traded with India and the Far East were incredibly rich.

Arabs played an important part in the history of exploration. In the 6th and 7th centuries they conquered a huge empire, spreading education and their religion, Islam.

Q What sort of ships did Arabs have?

A Arab ships were known as dhows. They had triangular sails, and needed only a small crew.

Q Where did Arab explorers learn about navigation?

A Arabs learned about navigation in the Indian Ocean while on trading missions. They worked out how to find their way by the stars. They also learned about tides, ocean currents and the monsoon cycle (heavy rainstorms).

Q Did Arab explorers make maps?

A Yes. There is a famous map of about 1150 made on a silver tablet by an explorer called Idrisi. He was a Spanish-born Arab who visited France and England as well as the East.

Early maps included only the top of Africa. The ship-like figure on the left is meant to show three lakes feeding into the River Nile.

Q Who was the greatest Arab explorer?

A The most famous Arab explorer was Ibn Batuta from Tangier in North Africa. He visited many countries from 1325 to 1355.

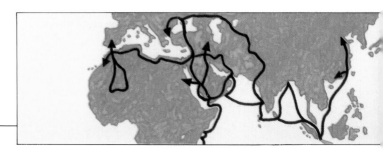

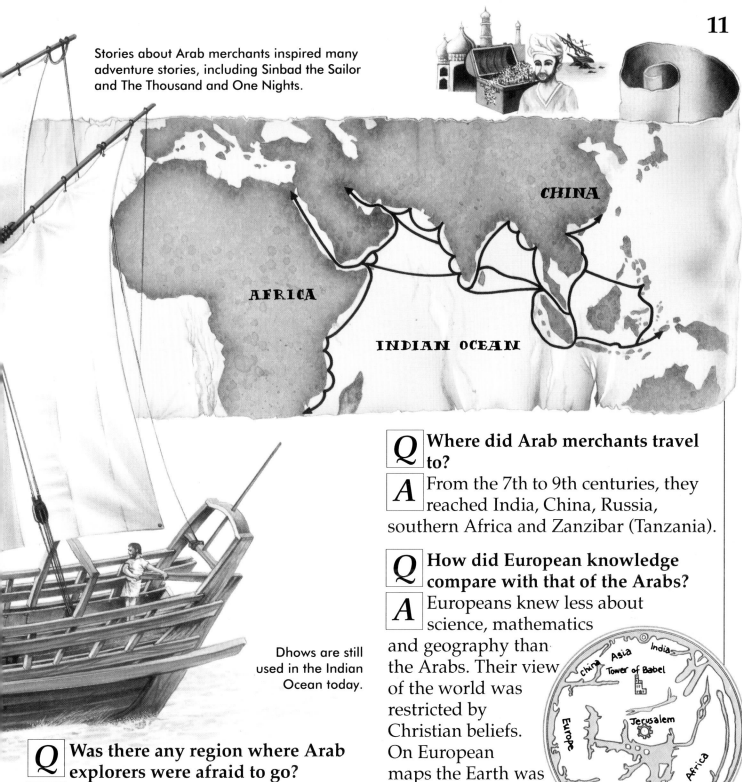

Stories about Arab merchants inspired many adventure stories, including Sinbad the Sailor and The Thousand and One Nights.

CHINA

AFRICA

INDIAN OCEAN

Dhows are still used in the Indian Ocean today.

Ibn Batuta travelled about 120,000km during his 30 years of voyages.

Q Where did Arab merchants travel to?

A From the 7th to 9th centuries, they reached India, China, Russia, southern Africa and Zanzibar (Tanzania).

Q How did European knowledge compare with that of the Arabs?

A Europeans knew less about science, mathematics and geography than the Arabs. Their view of the world was restricted by Christian beliefs. On European maps the Earth was shown as a circle with Jerusalem at its centre.

China · Asia · India · Tower of Babel · Europe · Jerusalem · Africa

Q Was there any region where Arab explorers were afraid to go?

A Arabs called the Atlantic 'The Sea of Darkness'. Idrisi may have sailed into it, but if he did he was the only Arab who dared to do so.

Q How did the West come to share Arab learning?

A Christian knights came into contact with the Arabs during the Crusades (1096-1291) when the Christians tried to win back Jerusalem. Arabs had also conquered much of Spain.

Marco Polo

Kublai Khan

Who first made contact with China?

China, in the Far East, was a difficult place to reach. In 1271 Marco Polo, the son of a merchant from Venice, Italy, travelled overland to Peking (Beijing) with his father and uncle and spent many years with the Chinese emperor Kublai Khan.

Q What did merchants want from the Chinese?

A Western merchants wanted silk, spices and porcelain which they traded in return for gold and silver.

Q Why did Marco Polo travel to China?

A Marco's father, Niccolo, and his uncle, Maffeo, had already spent 15 years in China. They returned to Italy and then, in 1271, decided to go back, taking Marco with them. They carried gifts from Pope Gregory X, who hoped the great Mongol leader Kublai Khan would recognize Christianity as superior to the many other religions in China.

Q How long did Marco stay in the Khan's court?

A The Khan kept Marco at his court for 17 years, sending him on diplomatic missions all over China. Because of his quick grasp of languages and his skill at making notes on everything he saw, Marco was able to report back to Kublai Khan and, later, to people in Venice.

Q Were the Polo family the first Europeans to reach China?

A No. The route known as the Silk Road, which ran from China to the West, had been used by traders since about 500 BC, but the Polos were the first Europeans to travel its entire length and make contact with Chinese leaders.

Venice

The Silk Road

Q How did the Polos travel to Shangdu, where Kublai Khan had his palace?

A They used camels to carry provisions through Armenia into Persia (Iran), through Afghanistan, the Gobi Desert and China. They travelled 11,200km, and took three and a half years to reach Shangdu. On the way they spent a year in Kanchow learning the customs of the Mongol peoples.

Junks were flat-bottomed ships with sails made of matting stiffened with wooden strips. They could make long voyages.

Q How did Marco return?

A Marco was given the job of escorting a princess to Persia (Iran), where she was to marry a prince. After stopping at Sumatra, Java, Malaya, Ceylon (Sri Lanka) and India, he delivered the princess to Persia and sailed home to Venice.

The Silk Road was so dangerous that goods were passed along it from one merchant to another. No-one before had travelled its entire length.

Shang-tu

PERSIA

The Chinese had already explored to the west. In the second century BC they reached Persia (Iran).

CHINA

Hormuz

Canton

INDIA

On his death bed, Marco Polo was asked to admit that he had been lying about his adventures. He replied "I have not told half of what I saw".

—— The Silk Road
- - - Marco Polo's Route

AFRICA

Q How did people learn of Marco's adventures?

A After Marco's return in 1295, war broke out between the Venetians and the Genoese, and he was taken prisoner. In prison he dictated his story to another prisoner. Many people did not believe his book, which described the discovery of oil, coal, magnificent palaces, parades of elephants, gifts to Kublai Khan of 100,000 white horses and huge jewels that were beyond the imagination of the Venetians.

Q What new sights did Marco see?

A On his travels Marco saw many strange and wonderful things unknown to Europeans. He marvelled at the huge cities and strange-shaped ships on the great rivers. He saw, for the first time, people using paper money, burning coal not wood, and printing words on paper using wooden blocks. Marco also found sources of jewels and spices.

When was the Great Age of Exploration?

The 15th and early 16th centuries are often called the Great Age of Exploration because so many discoveries were made at this time. Sea routes were found to the East, and unknown lands were explored - for example, America, the West Indies and the Pacific.

Q Why were there so many explorers at this time?

A This was an exciting time of new learning. Western Europeans wanted to find out more about the world, and had developed ships that would allow them to do so. Merchants wanted to obtain such valuable things as spices, silk, gems and fine china. Spices from the East were needed for cooking and medicines.

Q Which country began the Great Age of Exploration?

A The Portugese, in the early 15th century. Ships sailing out of Lisbon port picked up strong winds which drove them directly south until they picked up a wind to drive them east.

Q Who first sailed round the southern tip of Africa?

A The Portuguese captain, Bartolomeo Dias, in 1487. He had two caravels and a larger ship to carry stores. He sailed round the Cape of Good Hope but his crew refused to go any further.

Q Who paid for the expeditions?

A Usually they were sponsored by the royal family of a country. Prince Henry of Portugal became known as Henry the Navigator not because he ever went to sea, but because he sponsored Portuguese expeditions. Spanish and English kings and queens also paid for explorers' voyages. They wanted to find riches overseas and to gain power over any new lands that were discovered.

Q Which European first reached India by sea?

A The Portuguese sailor, Vasco da Gama. He followed Dias' route round Africa. Then he took on board an Arab pilot who helped him navigate to India. Da Gama lost two ships and half his men, but took back to Portugal a cargo of spices and precious gems.

Many of Da Gama's men died of scurvy from not having enough fresh food.

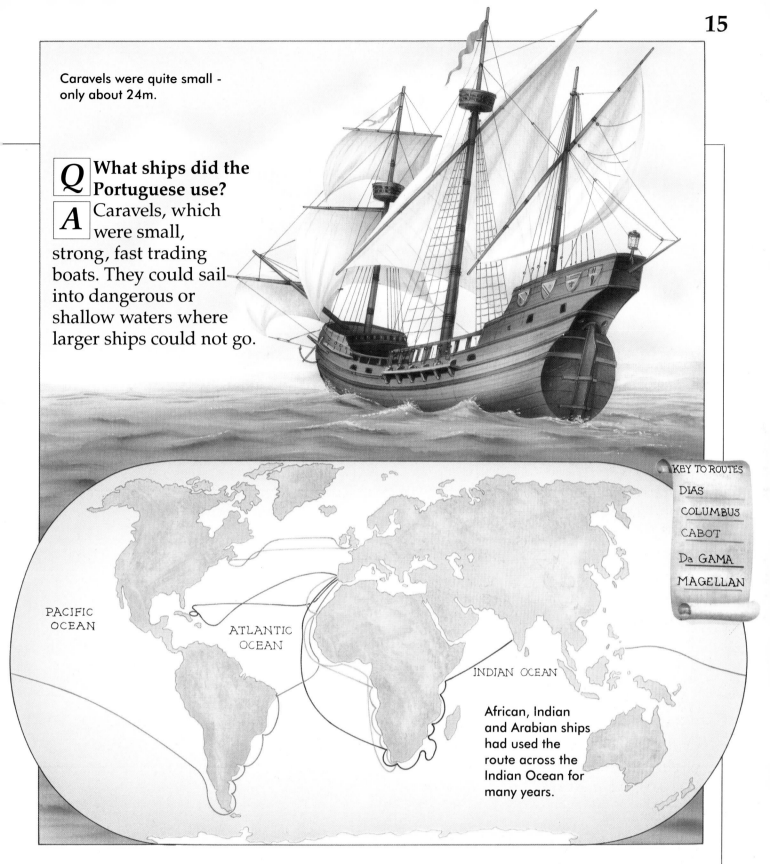

Caravels were quite small - only about 24m.

Q What ships did the Portuguese use?

A Caravels, which were small, strong, fast trading boats. They could sail into dangerous or shallow waters where larger ships could not go.

PACIFIC OCEAN

ATLANTIC OCEAN

INDIAN OCEAN

KEY TO ROUTES

DIAS

COLUMBUS

CABOT

Da GAMA

MAGELLAN

African, Indian and Arabian ships had used the route across the Indian Ocean for many years.

Q Which were the most exciting years of the Great Age of Exploration?

A These major discoveries were made within the astonishingly short space of 34 years:

1487 Dias sailed round the tip of Africa.
1492 Columbus reached the West Indies.
1497 The English explorer John Cabot reached Newfoundland, off North America.
1498 Da Gama reached India by sea.
1519-21 Magellan sailed into the Pacific.

In 1492 Christopher Columbus sailed from Spain across the Atlantic to the West Indies and found a 'New World' that nobody in Europe knew about. But people had been living in America for thousands of years before Europeans arrived.

Q **Was Columbus the first European to sail to America?**

A No. The Vikings had probably reached America in AD 985, but their voyages had been long forgotten when Columbus sailed.

Q **How many ships did Columbus take with him?**

A Columbus took three ships on his first voyage - the *Santa Maria* (his flagship), the *Nina* and the *Pinta*.

Columbus was a brave man. Da Gama knew that India existed, though he was not sure how to reach it. Columbus was sailing into the unknown.

The Santa Maria hit a coral reef in the West Indies, so only two ships made it back to Spain.

NORTH AMERICA

ATLANTIC OCEAN

WEST INDIES

Columbus found pearls in the West Indies which made him believe he had reached China as Marco Polo's book had mentioned the Chinese diving for them.

Q Where did Columbus believe he was going?

A He thought he was going to China. When he got to the West Indies he insisted they were islands off China.

Q What did Columbus expect to find?

A He expected to find gold, pearls and spices because they were all mentioned in Marco Polo's book on China.

Q Why were Columbus's crews frightened on the voyage?

A They thought they were going too far from home and that in the Atlantic no wind ever blew in the direction of Spain, so they might never return!

Q Where does the name 'America' come from?

A It comes from Amerigo Vespucci, an Italian adventurer, who claimed that he reached the mainland of America in 1497, but it is doubtful that he did so.

Q Did Columbus actually set foot in America?

A No. He first landed in the West Indies. Later, he made three more voyages to the West Indies. On his third voyage he reached Panama, in Central America, but he never landed on the mainland of North America.

Columbus believed the world was round, so you could reach the East by sailing west. His mistake was to think the world was smaller than it is. He thought the distance from Europe to Asia was 5713km. In fact it is 18,935km.

SPAIN

Palos

AFRICA

Each day Columbus lied to his men about the distance they had travelled because they were afraid of sailing too far from Spain.

Who first sailed around the world?

Ferdinand Magellan set out from Portugal in 1519, sailing westwards (like Columbus) to try to reach the East. He sailed down the coast of South America and round into the vast ocean which he named the Pacific.

Q Why didn't Magellan tell his men where they were going?

A He thought they would be too frightened to obey him. Many sailors were afraid of sea monsters.

Q How long were Magellan's men in the Pacific without fresh food?

A They spent three months and twenty days eating biscuits full of grubs and drinking stinking water. They also ate rats to survive..

Ferdinand Magellan

Many sailors died of hunger and disease because they did not have fresh food supplies.

Q How was the passage to the Pacific discovered?

A Two of Magellan's ships were blown in a storm towards the South American coast. Just in time the crews spotted a small opening. It was the strait (passage) they were looking for. It is now called the Strait of Magellan.

Q Did Magellan actually sail round the world?

A No, he was killed in a battle with islanders in the Philippines.

Q How many men returned safely?

A Of the 260 or so crew aboard five ships who set out, only 18 men and one ship, the *Vittoria*, returned to Spain in 1522. They were the first people to sail right round the world.

Q What 'strange' creatures did they see?

A In St Julian Bay, South America, Magellan's men described seeing strange birds, seawolves with webbed paws at their sides, and camels without humps. These were probably puffins, seals and llamas.

Q Who led the second voyage round the world?

A Sir Francis Drake, who left Britain in 1577 to rob Spanish treasure ships. Following Magellan's route round South America, he returned to England in 1580.

Sir Francis Drake

Who were the 'Conquistadors'?

Spaniards were appalled by the idol worship and human sacrifice they found in Mexico and Peru.

Once Columbus had successfully sailed across the Atlantic, Spaniards began to explore Central America. Adventurers came to the Americas to make their fortunes. These men became known as *Conquistadors* (which is Spanish for conquerors).

Q What did the Conquistadors want?

A They wanted land, gold and other riches. They also wanted to convert the native Americans to Christianity.

EMPIRE OF THE AZTECS

CENTRAL AMERICA

SOUTH AMERICA

EMPIRE OF THE INCAS

Cortes

Aztecs did not have horses or firearms. This helped Cortes to win.

Q Who already lived in South America?

A Many native peoples, including the Aztecs, who ruled in Mexico, and the Incas who ruled in Peru.

Q Who conquered the Aztecs?

A The Spaniard, Hernando Cortes, landed in Mexico in 1519 with 600 soldiers and 16 horses.

Aztecs thought one of their gods, Quetzalcoatl, had a white face and black beard - like Cortes. They believed he wore a feathered head-dress, and Cortes wore a feather in his helmet.

Spaniards took cows, horses and pigs to South America.

Q How did Cortes win with so few men?

A The Aztec emperor, Montezuma, thought that Cortes might be a god and so did not fight. Later, other tribes who did not like the Aztecs helped Cortes.

Thousands of Aztecs died of European diseases that the Spanish brought with them, such as smallpox, measles and colds.

Pizarro

Q What happened to the Incas?

A Another Spaniard, Francisco Pizarro, defeated the Incas in 1531-33 with a small army. He captured their king, said he would release him in return for a roomful of gold, then murdered the king anyway.

Red Pepper

Cacao Bean

Tomato

Potato

Turkey

When Drake returned to England in 1586, he brought news of tobacco, the Spanish name for a herb the Indians smoked.

Q What happened to the Aztecs?

A The Spaniards made the Aztecs slaves. They forced them to work hard in mines and on the land. Many died and within a few years the Aztec culture was destroyed.

Q What new items came to Europe from the New World?

A Tomatoes, chocolate (from the cacao bean) and red peppers came from America, as well as tobacco, potatoes and turkeys.

Who found out about Australia?

For a long time, geographers thought that there must be a southern continent to balance the weight of Europe and Asia, north of the Equator. They called this land Terra Australis Nondum Cognita (southern land not yet known).

Cook thought kangaroos looked like dogs, except that they jumped like hares.

Q Who first reached Australia?

A Aboriginal peoples have been living in Australia for thousands of years. The first European to sail there was a Dutch explorer, Willem Jansz, who reached the northern tip of Australia in 1606. Soon after, other Dutch ships explored the south seas, including, in 1642, Abel Tasman. He discovered Tasmania and went on to reach New Zealand.

Q Which explorers first saw kangaroos?

A Cook's crew saw kangaroos when the *Endeavour* ran aground off eastern Australia and took seven weeks to repair.

On long voyages, sailors usually got scurvy because they ate little fresh food and few vegetables. Cook made sure his men ate healthily.

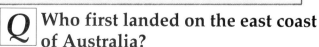

Q Who first landed on the east coast of Australia?

A Captain James Cook landed in 1770. The British Admiralty had sent him on a voyage of exploration.

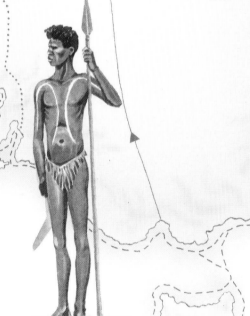

When Flinders got back, his ship was so rotten he could push a stick right through the bottom timbers.

Q **Who first sailed right round Australia?**

A A British naval officer, Matthew Flinders, between 1801 and 1803. He discovered how big Australia is, but his crew caught scurvy and his own health was damaged.

Q **Who first crossed Australia from south to north?**

A John Stuart, a Scotsman, crossed from Adelaide to Darwin in 1862. As a reward, he won a prize of £10,000 offered by the Australian government.

Stuart was so exhausted he had to be carried back in a sling tied between two horses.

In 1860, Robert Burke and Charles Wills had tried to cross Australia from south to north. They got within sound of the sea, but had to turn back and died on the way.

Q **Why did early settlers in the east keep to the coastal areas?**

A They could not find a way over the Blue Mountains, west of Sydney. In 1813, John Blaxland, William Lawson and William Wentworth got through by climbing the mountain ridges instead of following the valleys.

Q **How did the explorers treat the Aborigines?**

A They assumed Europeans were superior and so had a right to take the Aborigines' land. The Aboriginal lifestyle was soon almost destroyed.

FLINDER'S ROUTE

BURKE AND WILLS ROUTE

STUART'S ROUTE

Many explorers relied on Aborigines to help them find food and water.

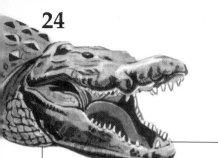

Who explored Africa?

Explorers faced fierce animals and dangerous conditions.

Africa is a huge continent that was first explored by Europeans in the 19th century. Its deserts, rivers, plains and jungles were uncharted, making journeys difficult and dangerous.

Q Why was Africa so dangerous for explorers?

A Africa was such a wild place that it took very determined explorers to brave the hazards. They had to put up with disease, fierce animals, rugged surroundings and often hostile people.

Livingstone was once attacked by a lion, he survived but was badly injured.

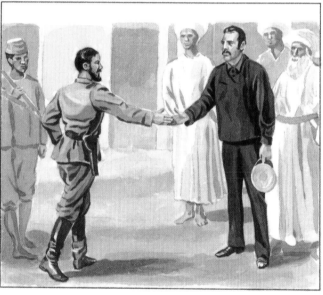

Q Who was the greatest explorer in Africa?

A The British explorer and missionary (spreader of Christianity) David Livingstone travelled nearly 50,000km through Africa from 1841 until his death in 1873. He went missing in 1866 and was not found again until 1871. He was found by the American explorer Henry Morton Stanley who used the famous greeting: "Doctor Livingstone, I presume?"

Q Who found the source of the River Nile?

A The River Nile is the longest river in the world. It flows for 6650km through North Africa to the Mediterranean Sea. John Hanning Speke, a British explorer, discovered in 1862 that the Nile flowed out of Lake Victoria.

The highest African mountain is Kilimanjaro (5895m) in Tanzania. A German, Hans Meyer, first reached the highest peak in 1889.

Q Who was the most famous woman explorer of Africa?

A In the 1890s a British woman, Mary Kingsley, explored West Africa and discovered many unknown species of birds and animals. She also fought for justice and medical care for the African people.

Q Who explored the Sahara Desert?

A The Sahara is the largest desert in the world with an area of 9 million sq km. One third of it is sand and the rest rocky wasteland. In the 1820s the Scottish explorers Hugh Clapperton and Walter Oudney, and English soldier Dixon Denham crossed the Sahara and made friends with Arab leaders.

Q What other great discoveries were made in Africa?

A The German explorer Heinrich Barth discovered the source of the River Niger in the 1850s and also discovered a new route across the Sahara Desert.

SAHARA

R. NIGER

R. NILE

Mt. KILIMANJARO

→▶ BARTH
········· STANLEY
———— LIVINGSTONE
– – – – SPEKE

How were polar regions explored?

On his journey to the North Pole, Robert Peary learned much from the Inuit (Eskimos) in his party.

ARCTIC OCEAN

NORTH
+
POLE

ALASKA

RUSSIA

GREENLAND

SOUTH
+
POLE
ANTARCTICA

The polar regions were only fully explored in the 20th century. Polar exploration is still difficult today but modern technology has made the task less hazardous.

Q What are the differences between the North and the South Poles?

A The North Pole is in the frozen Arctic Ocean, which is surrounded by inhabited lands such as Greenland, Alaska and Canada. The South Pole is in Antarctica, which is a vast uninhabited area of frozen land surrounded by sea.

Q Who first reached the North Pole?

A In 1909 an American naval officer, Robert Peary, and his team, reached the North Pole with supplies pulled by a team of huskies. He suffered severe frostbite and lost all his toes.

Q Who first reached the South Pole?

A In 1911 the Norwegian Roald Amundsen reached the South Pole just one month ahead of the British naval officer Robert Falcon Scott, who reached the Pole in January 1912. Scott and his four companions died during their return trip.

Q How did Amundsen beat Scott to the South Pole?

A Amundsen used dog teams (huskies) while Scott had ponies which could not stand the cold. Scott and his men ended up pulling their sledges themselves.

The boots of early polar explorers were sometimes stuffed with grass to keep their feet warm!

Q What did early polar explorers wear?

A Scott's team wore clothes made of cotton and wool which absorbed sweat, making them cold and wet. Amundsen's men wore furs and animal skins which let the body breathe as well as keeping it warm.

Q How do polar explorers keep warm today?

A They wear layers of clothes, trapping air between them. One layer is waterproof to stop sweat soaking outer layers of clothing. Outer clothes are windproof and padded.

Q What kind of shelters are needed?

A Tents are still used today but they are better insulated against the weather than those of the early explorers. Scientists working in polar regions for months at a time have proper buildings to work in.

Q What are the main dangers faced by polar explorers?

A Exposure (when the body is so chilled it cannot function) is the most serious hazard in polar cold. Frostbite, when the circulation of blood stops in fingers and toes, is another. Well-insulated clothes and warm food keep these at bay.

A search party found the bodies of Scott and his men in their tent eight months after they died.

How is the sea explored?

Underwater exploration reveals a strange and beautiful world. There are undersea mountains higher than any on the surface of the Earth, and millions of sea creatures. On the sea bed there are many ancient shipwrecks.

Q Why explore the sea bed?

A Scientists want to discover more about the Earth's structure and life on the sea bed. There are also valuable minerals, such as oil, under the sea. Some explorers are interested in shipwrecks and the cargo they carried.

Q What is a diving bell?

A It is an early underwater exploration device. Air from the surface was pumped into a bell-shaped container. A diver could sit inside it and explore under the sea, but could not go very deep.

Q How can people explore great depths?

A Special underwater craft have been designed. For example, Frenchman Auguste Piccard and his son Jacques designed a deep-diving craft called a bathyscaphe. In 1960 Jacques took the bathyscaphe *Trieste* down to a depth of 11km under the Pacific Ocean. It took five hours to reach the sea bed. There are also small submarines, called submersibles, that can dive as deep as 6000m.

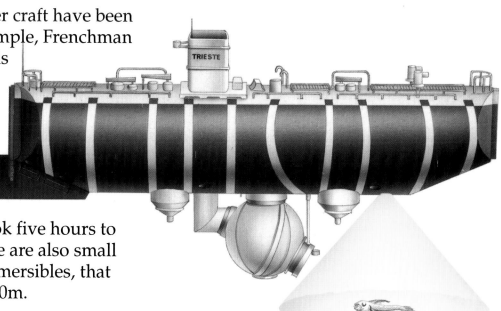

In the deepest parts of the oceans it is very cold and there is no light. Even so, some creatures are found living there.

Submersibles work from and return to a 'mother ship' on the surface.

Q What is an aqualung?

A It is an underwater breathing device invented in 1943 by the French. Cylinders of compressed air are fastened to the diver's back and a tube feeds the air to a mouthpiece. With this, divers can safely descend to a depth of about 73m, carrying their air supply with them.

Q What do underwater robots do?

A Underwater search robots have been developed. They were used to explore the sunken remains of ships such as the *Titanic* and the *Bismark*. The robots are controlled from the surface, so human lives are not put at risk.

Q How do scientists map the sea floor?

A They use echo-sounding equipment to chart the shape of the sea bed. This works like radar, bouncing sound waves off objects.

Underwater robots can collect samples and relay television pictures to the surface.

How is space explored?

The Russian word for astronaut is 'cosmonaut'. In 1963 the first woman in space was cosmonaut Valentina Tereshkova.

Space explorers use shuttles and robot craft to investigate the solar system and beyond. Scientists learn more every day about planets and stars through the pictures and information sent back to earth.

Q When was the first rocket invented?

A The Chinese invented gunpowder which they used to fire the first rockets in 1232.

Q Who was the first person to travel in a rocket?

A An un-named woman pilot during the Second World War (1939-45) tested a German rocket that was capable of travelling long distances.

Q Who was the first person in space?

A The first person to leave the Earth's atmosphere in a rocket was a Russian, Yuri Gagarin. He made one orbit of Earth on 12 April 1961, in Vostok 1. The flight lasted 1 hour and 48 minutes.

Q What is a space shuttle?

A A shuttle is a vehicle sent into space attached to a rocket. After leaving the rocket it is used to complete tasks in space, such as launching satellites. Then the shuttle is flown back to Earth to be used again.

Space shuttles land on a runway just like large gliders.

WHAT MAKES A DEGAS A DEGAS?

Richard Mühlberger

The Metropolitan Museum of Art
CHERRYTREE BOOKS

A Cherrytree Book
First published in 1993 by The Metropolitan Museum of Art, New York, and Viking, a division of Penguin Books USA Inc.
Copyright © 1993 by The Metropolitan Museum of Art
What Makes a . . . a . . . ? is a trademark of The Metropolitan Museum of Art.

This edition first published in 1994 by Cherrytree Press Ltd, Windsor Bridge Road, Bath, Avon BA2 3AX.
Copyright © Cherrytree Press Ltd, 1994.

Produced by the Department of Special Publications,
The Metropolitan Museum of Art
Series Editor: Mary Beth Brewer
Front Cover Design: Marleen Adlerblum
Design: Nai Y. Chang
Printing and Binding: A. Mondadori, Verona, Italy

British Library Cataloguing in Publication Data
Mühlberger, Richard
What Makes a Degas a Degas?
I. Title
759.4

ISBN 0-7451-5248-1 Hardcover
ISBN 0-7451-5226-0 Softcover

All rights reserved. No part of this publication may be reproduced, stored in a retrieval system, or transmitted, in any form or by any means without the prior permission in writing of the copyright holder, nor be otherwise circulated in any form of binding or cover other than that in which it is published and without a similar condition including this condition being imposed on the subsequent purchaser.

ILLUSTRATIONS

Unless otherwise noted, all works are by Edgar Degas and in oil on canvas.

Pages 1 and 2: *The Dance Class*, 83 × 77 cm ($32\frac{3}{4} \times 30\frac{1}{4}$ in.), 1874, The Metropolitan Museum of Art, Bequest of Mrs. Harry Payne Bingham, 1986, 1987.47.1.

Page 6: *Self-Portrait*, oil on paper, laid down on canvas, 41 × 34 cm ($16 \times 13\frac{1}{2}$ in.), The Metropolitan Museum of Art, Bequest of Stephen C. Clark, 1960, 61.101.6.

Page 8: *Study of a Draped Figure*, graphite heightened with white gouache on beige paper, 29 × 23 cm ($11\frac{1}{2} \times 8\frac{7}{8}$ in.), The Metropolitan Museum of Art, Rogers Fund, 1975, 1975.5.

Page 8: Jean Auguste Dominique Ingres, *Study of Classical Drapery*, black chalk, estompe, partially squared off in black chalk, on beige paper, 49 × 32 cm ($19\frac{3}{8} \times 12\frac{5}{8}$ in.), The Metropolitan Museum of Art, Gustavus A. Pfeiffer Fund, 1963, 63.66.

Page 9: *At the Milliner's*, pastel on pale grey wove paper, adhered to silk bolting in 1951, 76 × 86 cm (30 × 34 in.), 1882, The Metropolitan Museum of Art, H. O. Havemeyer Collection, Bequest of Mrs. H. O. Havemeyer, 1929, 29.100.38.

Page 10: *The Bellelli Family*, 200 × 250 cm ($78\frac{3}{4} \times 98\frac{3}{8}$ in.), 1858-67, Musée d'Orsay, Paris, © PHOTO R.M.N.

Page 13: *Giulia Bellelli*, essence on buff wove paper mounted on panel, 38 × 27 cm ($15\frac{1}{8} \times 10\frac{1}{2}$ in.), Dumbarton Oaks Research Library and Collections, Washington, D.C.

Page 14: *A Woman Seated Beside a Vase of Flowers (Madame Paul Valpinçon?)*, 74 × 93 cm ($29 \times 36\frac{1}{2}$ in.), 1865, The Metropolitan Museum of Art, H. O. Havemeyer Collection, Bequest of Mrs. H. O. Havemeyer, 1929, 29.100.128.

Page 19: *Carriage at the Races*, 37 × 56 cm ($14\frac{3}{8} \times 22$ in.), 1931 Purchase Fund, Courtesy, Museum of Fine Arts, Boston.

Page 21: Utagawa Hiroshige, *Mochizuki Station*, from the series *The Sixty-nine Post Stations of the Kisokaido*, colour woodblock print, 25 × 38 cm ($9\frac{3}{4} \times 14\frac{7}{8}$ in.), ca. 1835, The Metropolitan Museum of Art, Purchase, Joseph Pulitzer Bequest, 1918, JP 585.

Page 22: *The Orchestra of the Opéra*, 57 × 46 cm ($22\frac{1}{4} \times 18\frac{1}{4}$ in.), Musée d'Orsay, Paris, © PHOTO R.M.N.

Page 25: *The Ballet from 'Robert le Diable'*, 66 × 55 cm ($26 \times 21\frac{3}{8}$ in.), 1872, The Metropolitan Museum of Art, H. O. Havemeyer Collection, Bequest of Mrs. H. O. Havemeyer, 1929, 29.100.552.

Page 26: *Race Horses at Longchamp*, 34 × 42 cm ($13\frac{3}{8} \times 16\frac{1}{2}$ in.), S. A. Denio Collection, Courtesy, Museum of Fine Arts, Boston.

Page 28: *Portraits in an Office (New Orleans)*, 73 × 92 cm ($28\frac{3}{4} \times 36\frac{1}{4}$ in.), 1873, Musée des Beaux-Arts, Pau; photograph, Marie-Louise Perony, Pau.

Page 33: *The Dance Class*, 83 × 77 cm ($32\frac{3}{4} \times 30\frac{1}{4}$ in.), 1874, The Metropolitan Museum of Art, Bequest of Mrs. Harry Payne Bingham, 1986, 1987.47.1.

Page 34: *Sketch of a Ballet Dancer*, brush and india ink on pink paper, 31 × 44 cm ($12\frac{3}{8} \times 17\frac{1}{2}$ in.), The Metropolitan Museum of Art, Robert Lehman Collection, 1975, 1975.1.611, recto.

Page 34: *Two Dancers*, dark brown wash and white gouache on bright pink commercially coated wove paper now faded to pale pink, 61 × 39 cm ($24\frac{1}{8} \times 15\frac{1}{2}$ in.), 1873, The Metropolitan Museum of Art, H. O. Havemeyer Collection, Bequest of Mrs. H. O. Havemeyer, 1929, 29.100.187.

Page 35: *Seated Dancer*, graphite and charcoal heightened with white on pink wove paper, squared for transfer, 42 × 33 cm ($16\frac{3}{8} \times 12\frac{7}{8}$ in.), The Metropolitan Museum of Art, H. O. Havemeyer Collection, Bequest of Mrs. H. O. Havemeyer, 1929, 29.100.942.

Page 35: *The Ballet Master, Jules Perrot*, oil on brown wove paper, 48 × 30 cm ($18\frac{15}{16} \times 11\frac{15}{16}$ in.), 1875, Philadelphia Museum of Art, The Henry P. McIlhenny Collection in Memory of Frances P. McIlhenny.

Page 36: *Miss La La at the Cirque Fernando*, 117 × 77 cm ($46 \times 30\frac{1}{2}$ in.), 1879, reproduced by courtesy of the Trustees, The National Gallery, London.

Page 37: *Study for Miss La La* at *the Cirque Fernando*, black chalk and pastel, 47 × 32 cm ($18\frac{1}{2} \times 12\frac{1}{2}$ in.), 1879, The Barber Institute of Fine Arts, The University of Birmingham.

Page 38: *A Woman Ironing*, 54 × 39 cm ($21\frac{3}{8} \times 15\frac{1}{2}$ in.), 1873, The Metropolitan Museum of Art, H. O. Havemeyer Collection, Bequest of Mrs. H. O. Havemeyer, 1929, 29.100.46.

Page 39: *Woman Ironing*, 81 × 66 cm (32 × 26 in.), Collection of Mr. and Mrs. Paul Mellon, © 1993 National Gallery of Art, Washington.

Page 41: *The Singer in Green*, pastel on light blue laid paper, 60 × 46 cm ($23\frac{3}{4} \times 18\frac{1}{4}$ in.),The Metropolitan Museum of Art, Bequest of Stephen C. Clark, 1960, 61.101.7.

Page 43: *The Millinery Shop*, 100 × 111 cm ($39\frac{3}{8} \times 43\frac{5}{8}$ in.), 1879–84, Mr. and Mrs. Lewis Larned Coburn Memorial Collection, 1933.428; photograph © 1992, The Art Institute of Chicago. All Rights Reserved.

Page 44: *Dancers, Pink and Green*, 82 × 76 cm ($32\frac{3}{8} \times 29\frac{3}{4}$ in.), The Metropolitan Museum of Art, H. O. Havemeyer Collection, Bequest of Mrs. H. O. Havemeyer, 1929, 29.100.42.

Page 47: *Self-Portrait* (?), photograph, The Metropolitan Museum of Art, Gift of Mrs. Henry T. Curtiss, 1964, 64.673.7.

Page 49: *The Rehearsal of the Ballet Onstage*, oil colours, freely mixed with turpentine, with traces of watercolour and pastel over pen-and-ink drawing on cream-coloured wove paper, laid on bristol board, mounted on canvas, 54 × 73 cm ($21\frac{3}{8} \times 28\frac{3}{4}$ in.), The Metropolitan Museum of Art, H. O. Havemeyer Collection, Gift of Horace Havemeyer, 1929, 29.160.26.

CONTENTS

SELF-PORTRAIT

Meet Edgar Degas

Hilaire Germain Edgar Degas was born on 19 July 1834, in Paris, France. He had an American-born mother from New Orleans, Louisiana, and a half-French father from Naples, Italy. Degas' father was a banker who considered it essential to expose his son to music and art. Known from the start as Edgar, the future painter attended an élite boarding school for boys named the Lycée Louis-le-Grand. Soon after he left school he announced that he wanted to be a painter, causing a major rift with his father.

Degas then went off on his own and lived a life of great poverty in an attic room. He so impressed his father with his seriousness that they made up their quarrel, and from then on Degas always had the full support of his parents. He attended art school in Paris, and then travelled around Italy, where he drew copies of the great paintings and sculptures of the past. This was the traditional way to complete a course of study in art.

Degas forged enduring friendships at school and was always loyal to his family. He made another, informal family of schoolmates from the Lycée Louis-le-Grand and artist friends. To them, he was as famous for his cantankerous personality and complaining as he was for his spectacular talent for drawing and painting.

The Old Master of the Impressionists

Degas is celebrated as one of the French Impressionists, an informal group of artistic revolutionaries that included Claude Monet, Berthe Morisot, Camille Pissarro and Pierre Auguste Renoir. When he was young, Degas enjoyed spending hours with his friends talking about art. He helped organize their exhibitions, hung his paintings with theirs and respected their concern for painting subjects from everyday life. But he did not accompany them on painting excursions. The Impressionists painted out of doors; Degas preferred working in his studio. They usually painted quickly; he was much slower. They enjoyed landscapes; he painted very few. They liked spontaneity; he liked to plan. They worked directly on their canvases with paint; he prepared detailed drawings on paper before he painted anything. They did not even share the same heroes in art.

Degas forever sought to learn the techniques of the Italian Renaissance artists Leonardo da Vinci, Raphael and Michelangelo, and other

STUDY OF A DRAPED FIGURE

Degas admired Ingres above all other artists, and he practised drawing in his idol's style. Figures like these resemble Greek statues, which were considered to embody the highest ideals of beauty.

Jean Auguste Dominique Ingres
STUDY OF CLASSICAL DRAPERY

celebrated artists of the past. As a young man, he met Jean Auguste Dominique Ingres, a painter fifty-four years his senior, who worked in this tradition. Ingres drew with solid, graceful lines. Seeing Ingres' work increased Degas' belief that drawing must be the foundation of his own art. In this, he sided with older generations instead of with his young contemporaries, who expressed themselves more with colour than with line. After a few tries at painting classical themes, such as scenes set in ancient Greece, he curbed the impulse to imitate the subjects that his heroes had painted, realizing that they were out of date. Instead, Degas began specializing in scenes of modern life, allying himself more closely with his Impressionist friends.

Degas always bridged two worlds, the fresh, new world of Impressionism and the solid, traditional one of the Old Masters. Perhaps he would not have called himself an Impressionist, but he probably would have enjoyed being known as the Old Master of the Impressionist group.

AT THE MILLINER'S

Modern life was a new subject for nineteenth-century artists. In paintings like this, the viewer sees an everyday place like a hat shop from the artist's point of view.

9

The Bellelli Family

Even as a young man, Edgar Degas excelled at certain things. None of his contemporaries, for example, could match him in portrait painting. When Degas complained that he was bored with painting people's faces, his father urged him on. He insisted to his son that 'portraiture will be the finest jewel in your crown'. During the first two decades of the artist's career, nearly half of his paintings were portraits, mainly of his family and himself. Degas set out to capture not only appearances, but also personality traits, and he succeeded. His first great masterpiece was the disturbingly frank portrayal of his aunt Laura with her daughters and husband. The painting is called *The Bellelli Family*.

Degas' aunt, Laura Degas Bellelli, stands in a regal and protective way, staring sadly past her children and husband. Ten-year-old Giovanna, restrained by her mother's hand on her shoulder, crosses her hands nervously and stares straight ahead. Her seven-year-old sister, Giulia, screws her fists to her waist and looks towards her father. Arranged in a triangle, and dressed in black and white, they form a strong, united group. Baron Gennaro Bellelli is shown apart from them, next to the desk and in front of the fireplace. Degas had the gift of catching candid moments. He pictured the family not posing, but getting ready to pose, for a portrait.

Degas said that he experimented with tones of black and white in the painting. His aunt's father had just died, so Laura Bellelli was dressed in mourning. The death also explains the black dresses her daughters wear. Degas placed a portrait of the dead man prominently on the wall next to his aunt. On the far left is a baby's crib draped in white, for the baroness is pregnant. There is also a white candle on the mantel, waiting to be lit. Degas echoed its shape and colour in Giulia's one exposed leg. Perhaps he thought the girls and the crib represented light and new life, a happy

thought amid a black cloud of unhappiness that had long hung over the family.

The Bellelli family had been expelled from Naples, their home city, because of Baron Bellelli's revolutionary activities. After almost nine years of living in exile, the family returned to Italy and rented a furnished apartment in Florence. In 1858, Degas visited them there. The artist probably never saw his relatives together as he eventually pictured them. Instead, he drew and painted them individually and in groups, and later referred to these studies as he pieced together a composition for his final large canvas. Most of the work was done in Paris.

Living far from home and in much poorer circumstances than they had been accustomed to, the family seems uncomfortable in its new surroundings. Degas lived in the apartment with the Bellellis during his stay in Florence, so he was acutely aware of the tensions his relatives were experiencing. He chose to show them silent, withdrawn, and detached from one another.

OPPOSITE:
GIULIA BELLELLI
In preparation for his paintings, Degas made numerous sketches and drawings. They helped him decide how everything would look in the finished work. Here he concentrated on the posture of his cousin. He may or may not have instructed her to rest her hands at her sides, but it seems like a natural pose for an active girl trying to sit still for her portrait. But when set into the complete family portrait, the turn of her head and position of her hands seem to be a reaction to her strict mother.

1865

A Woman Seated Beside a Vase of Flowers

It is not unusual to see a painting of a woman with a vase of flowers nearby. But here Degas painted just the opposite. The flowers appear in the centre, and the woman leans into the picture from the side. It is assumed that she picked the flowers from the garden that can be glimpsed through the window by her head. The gloves she wore to protect her hands are on the table next to a glass jug half filled with water. Having finished her first task of the day, and slightly weary from it, the woman rests, content to think and plan in solitude.

The luxuriousness of the flowers sets the theme for Degas. He filled more than half the picture with the blooms. Behind them, the wallpaper has a less brilliant, flatter floral design. Even the cloth that covers the table is decorated with flowers. In the background, dabs of pale colour indicate flowers blooming in the garden, which can be seen through the curtained window. Throughout the painting, Degas created rich textures by making the flowers small and keeping them close together. The woman's dress is also textured, with waves of light and dark that make it look like crushed suede. Her hat and dress blend with the other colours in the picture. The only plain areas of the painting stand out: the woman's hand and face and the black scarf round her neck.

Through a Keyhole

At first glance, it may seem that the flowers are the primary subject of the painting, but after a second look, there is no doubt that the subject is the woman. Although she is partly hidden by the corner of the table, and the frame cuts off most of her left shoulder, arm and hand, her presence is large. A spirited disposition and clever mind are suggested in the curve of her fingers, the position of her hand and the way she is looking. Degas drew attention to the woman in an odd and daring way: by placing her almost out of the picture.

Degas wanted it to seem as though he and the viewer had just walked into the room where the woman is sitting. Later in his life, Degas said he liked his figures to look as though they had been seen through a keyhole. The feeling of immediacy became a hallmark of Degas' art. However, he was always quick to say, 'Art was never less spontaneous than mine,' an acknowledgement that his 'candid' views were, in fact, very complex tricks. Nor was he ever known to paint a scene on the spot. *A Woman Seated Beside a Vase of Flowers* was composed in the traditional way, in his studio, from drawings.

OVERLEAF:
Here Degas contrasts the lively and dynamic flowers with the subdued and introspective attitude of the woman. We do not know what she is thinking as she turns away from the flowers.

15

Carriage at the Races

Paul Valpinçon was Degas' best friend at school and remained close to the artist all his life. Degas was a frequent visitor to his country house in Normandy, the northwest region of France. Normandy was very different from Paris. Degas thought that the countryside was 'exactly like England', and seeing horses on the farms there inspired him to paint equestrian subjects. During a visit in 1869, however, Degas found horses secondary to Paul Valpinçon's infant son, Henri. This becomes apparent when you look closely at the painting *Carriage at the Races*.

At first, Degas' composition seems lop-sided. In one corner are the largest and darkest objects, a pair of horses and a carriage. Against the lacquered body of the carriage, the creamy white tones of the passengers stand out. They are framed by the dark colours rather than overwhelmed by them.

Degas placed a cream-coloured parasol in the middle of the painting shading some of the figures in the carriage. Near it, balanced on the back of the driver's seat, is a black bulldog. Paul Valpinçon himself is the driver. Both Paul and the dog are gazing at the baby, who lies in the shade of the parasol. With pink, dimpled knees, Henri, not yet a year old, sprawls on the lap of his nurse while his mother looks on.

Ideas from the Exotic, Old and New

Degas always enjoyed looking at art. One of the thrills of his school years was being allowed to inspect the great paintings in the collection of Paul Valpinçon's father. Throughout his life, the artist drew inspiration from the masterpieces in the Louvre in Paris, one of the greatest museums in the world. He also found ideas in Japanese

By cutting off, or cropping, the carriage on the left, Degas created the impression that the viewer is on the spot, glancing at the scene for the first time.

prints. They were considered cheap, disposable souvenirs in Japan, but were treasured by artists and others in the West as highly original, fascinating works of art. Photography, a recent invention, also suggested to Degas ways of varying his paintings. He eventually became an enthusiastic photographer himself.

In *Carriage at the Races*, the way in which the horses and carriage are cut off recalls figures in photographs and Japanese prints. For Degas, showing only part of a subject made his paintings more intimate, immediate and realistic. He wanted viewers to see the scene as if they were actually there.

Utagawa Hiroshige
MOCHIZUKI STATION
In Japanese prints, objects and figures were often arranged diagonally and cut off at the edge. Prints like this one inspired Degas to position important features in his paintings so that they were partly cut off by the frame.

The Orchestra of the Opéra

Few of Degas' many portraits were painted just for money. He mostly painted people he knew and liked, and this familiarity encouraged him to try new approaches. Désiré Dihau, the bassoon player in the orchestra of the Paris Opéra, asked Degas to paint him. He was Degas' friend and a frequent guest at the house of Degas' father at evenings devoted to music. Degas thought a great deal about how the portrait should look, discarding the idea of showing the bassoonist alone on a canvas. Instead, the artist decided to show him at work in the orchestra pit during a performance at the Opéra. The result is the illusion of a real moment in the musician's life.

The face of every man in the painting has been identified. Some were Opéra musicians, and others were friends of the artist, none of whom knew how to play an instrument. Degas made the non-musicians look authentic by using characteristic poses he learned from watching the orchestra play during many years of Opéra performances. Not only did Degas' painting make musicians out of men who were not, it also rearranged the orchestra's traditional seating. Usually, Mr Dihau's chair would be off to the left, behind the cellos and double basses. Here, he sits in front and in the centre. Degas once made a note to himself to some day paint the 'swelling out and hollowing of the cheeks of the bassoonist'. In

this painting, he convincingly caught Mr Dihau's controlled breath as well as his practised fingers.

Linking Dancers and Musicians

Degas portrayed a dozen or more men, all packed closely into the left side of the orchestra pit. One slanting line separates them from the audience, and another, from the stage. Both lines slope down to the right. The angle of the bassoon points up to the man at the far right who plays the double bass. The scroll of this instrument, in turn, links the men below to the women on the

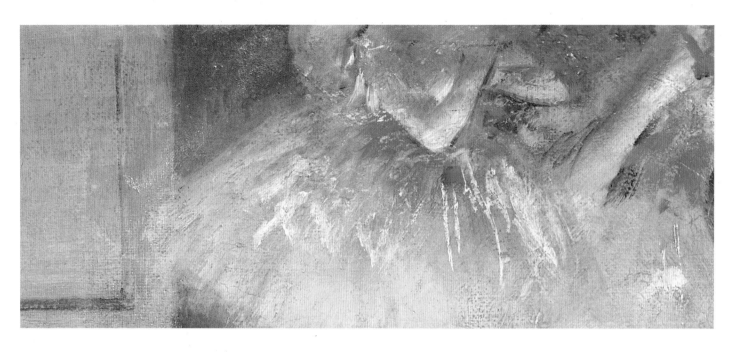

stage. All the players wear formal dress, yet the bright white of Mr Dihau's starched collar, tie and shirtfront calls special attention to him. Though the top of Mr Dihau's bassoon is hidden by the shoulder of the double bass player and the bottom of it is behind the divider, Degas showed more of his friend's instrument than anyone else's. This lively peek-a-boo view of the orchestra gives a much stronger sense of being there than it would have if every face and instrument had been arranged without over-lapping.

Degas became famous for his pictures of ballet dancers, and this is the very first he

painted. The dancers seem to be present here less for their beauty and grace than to provide a contrast to the musicians. The most obvious contrast is startling: The legs of the men do not show, but just the opposite is true of the women, whose heads and shoulders are cut off. The black wool and white linen of the men's clothing set off the dancers' pink and blue tulle. The light that illuminates the orchestra contrasts with the footlights on the stage. The brightest area of the dance is immediately above Mr Dihau, and the deepest bend of a dancing leg perfectly imitates the angle at which he holds his bassoon.

THE BALLET FROM 'ROBERT LE DIABLE'
Mr Dihau is less conspicuous in this painting than in the orchestra portrait painted by Degas three years earlier. The bassoon player is in his usual seat, his profile silhouetted against a page of music.

Race Horses at Longchamp

Plaster sculptures of horses showing the animals' bones and muscles were often found in the large studios where art students worked. These models may have guided Degas in his first drawings of horses. Also, he rode frequently and thus knew, as he put it, 'the difference between a thoroughbred and a half-bred'. French enthusiasm for thoroughbred horses was recent and fashionable, and in Degas' lifetime horse racing became as popular as it was in England. Degas became a distinguished painter of race horses, and he painted them many times.

On the western outskirts of Paris there is a large forest called the Bois de Boulogne. In 1856, a strip of land in the forest was given over to horse racing. It is called the Hippodrome de Longchamp. In this painting, Degas shows the racetrack at dusk. Following his usual method of constructing paintings in his studio, he based the images of the animals and their jockeys on drawings he had made a few years before. In fact, he often used the same drawing for a number of paintings. His skill hides his method. Here, the viewer is convinced that Degas was actually on the grass at Longchamp at the end of a racing day, watching the jockeys ride their mounts back to the stables.

Degas viewed the scene as though he were behind the horses on the right. By putting the stretch of trees between the jockeys' heads and the evening sky, he created an up-and-down play of colours. Degas repeated the pale yellow, blue and pink from the sky in the shirts and caps of the jockeys. The soft light of dusk makes the colours glow. Degas gave each jockey the colours that best unify the various parts of the painting. He wanted the viewer's eye to go from the blue chevron-striped sleeves on the right to the blue caps and shirts on the left, and to find the patterns of white that link the riders with the stanchions marking the racecourse.

An Empathy for Horses

Degas was sensitive to the moods of horses. The patterns he created with the animals' legs against the turf emphasize the relaxed gait of the slow-moving creatures. They have done their work for the day and the pleasures of feeding and grooming lie ahead. The horse on the far left, however, shies. Degas originally painted its legs in another position before deciding to show it pulling to the left. The earlier paint marks still show, producing an animated effect rather like the double exposure of a photograph.

Portraits in an Office (New Orleans)

The American Relatives

Degas' mother had many relatives in New Orleans. They lured the artist's two brothers there to start a business, and Degas visited them in 1872. He travelled by paddle steamer from England to New York, and then continued by train for four days. His trip was as interesting to him as the city itself. 'Everything attracts me here. I look at everything,' he wrote to a friend in France. It is not known whether he painted anything other than portraits of the relatives he had come to see. He described them as 'very affectionate but a bit free and easy with you, and who take you much less seriously because you are their nephew or their cousin.'

Cotton was the business of his New Orleans relatives, and Degas discovered that they were engrossed by it. 'One does nothing here . . . nothing but cotton, one lives for cotton and from cotton,' Degas wrote. While he was visiting his uncle's offices one day, samples of cotton arrived from a plantation up the Mississippi river. This gave Degas the idea for the major project of his four-and-a-half-month stay in America. The painting that resulted, *Portraits in an Office*, turned out to be one of his most famous.

Degas viewed his uncle's office from one corner. In the upper left, a silvery rectangle marks one end of the long office. At the other end of the room is a tall panel of eighteen rectangular panes of glass, shining like mirrors. In between, the rhythmic patterns of glass panes, mullions and frames march along the wall, turn the corner, and continue on, enclosing an inner office where two men work. The theme of rectangular patterns within a rectangular space continues in the shelves full of cotton samples at the far end of the office, in the fireplace, and in the frame of a painting of a ship that hangs above it. Every one of these straight-edged shapes is surrounded by the seafoam green of the walls and the warm shades of the floor and ceiling.

Recognition for the New Orleans Masterpiece

Degas told a close artist friend that the office interior scene was 'a fairly vigorous picture'. He could not have meant its mood or subject, because they are as relaxed as life in the American South. What must have been vigorous for Degas was fitting fourteen people into one canvas so all their faces would show! He used a trick learned from Japanese prints to make room for his assembled relatives and their chief employees and customers. He elevated the floor slightly from the far end of the office, which allowed everyone's head to show. Placing some of the men in chairs and some standing also made it easier to arrange their faces and bodies into a realistic-looking scene.

Degas used the white of the clothing, paper and cotton to lead the viewer's eye to critical areas in the office. His white paint is sometimes pure, and sometimes tinged with other colours. In each case, he used black close by to make the white seem whiter. The white cuffs and collar nearest the front of the scene belong to Degas'

uncle, the man in the top hat testing cotton. The white newspaper held by one of the artist's brothers is set against his dark clothing. Behind this figure, gathered around a long rectangle of cotton on a table, are the men who buy and sell the cotton. Degas put his second brother in shadows. With his legs crossed, he leans against the wall on the far left of the picture. A man less important to Degas, but essential to his family's cotton exchange, is the accountant on the far right. He wears the brightest white in the painting, and he is the largest figure in it. He is also conspicuous because of the detailed still life Degas made of his account books and wastepaper basket. Near them the artist decided to place his signature, the name of the city, New Orleans (using *Nlle*, the abbreviation in French for 'new'), and the date, 1873.

Before the paint was dry, Degas returned to France. He hoped very much that his painting would be purchased by someone who would appreciate it, but for five years no one showed any interest. Finally, the work was shown in an exhibition in the small city of Pau, in the south-west corner of France near the Spanish border. The town's art museum then bought it. Degas wrote immediately to the museum's curator, 'I must offer my warmest thanks for the honour you have done me. I must also admit that it is the first time that a museum has so honoured me and that this official recognition comes as a surprise and is terribly flattering.'

The Dance Class

Degas became the outstanding painter of dancers of his time, and few have ever matched him in painting the fine detail of ballet preparation and performance. At about the time he was getting ready to paint *The Dance Class* and other dance scenes, Degas met one of the greatest male dancers and choreographers, Jules Perrot. His strength and grace dominated the ballet stages of France and Russia in the 1830s and 1840s, and by the time Degas became a painter, Perrot was a renowned dance teacher.

Degas drew detailed studies of his new friend. They show the sixty-four-year-old man in a characteristic pose of a dance master, standing with legs astride, hands resting on a stout staff, and an experienced, critical expression on his face. Degas had made a great number of sketches of ballet dancers in every conceivable pose, and from these he created an imaginary class for the great teacher.

Degas could have posed Mr Perrot at an actual class at the Opéra, but he did not. His way of making pictures was not to capture the whole thing at once on the spot. That was the job of the photographer, he would have said. He preferred to imagine his picture, then make it come alive through a careful use of his drawings. Here he had to overlap figures that in his drawings appeared in their entirety, as well as change the sizes of figures so they would look convincing in the long practice room. The mirror in the middle focuses attention on Mr Perrot. As the teacher stares at the dancer practising before him, his expression and stance suggest that he is mentally noting ways in which his student can improve her technique.

Tricks of Composition

The five dancers close to the front of the painting are considerably larger than the dancing figure halfway back, yet they do not take attention away from her. Along with the music stand and the cello on the floor, they form a large in-and-out pattern. In the background, hands on hips, a dark-haired dancer stands on a platform, gazing out towards the dancing demonstration. Degas transformed the cluster of human beings and attractive objects at which the eye would usually stop into a pattern that instead moves the eye on. This pattern supplements his use of the bright mirror to direct the eye to the dancer and the dance master. These composition techniques are augumented by a device guaranteed to bring the viewer to the middle of the painting: Degas left half the floor empty. Anyone who wishes can walk right up to Mr Perrot and his student, if not with the feet, then certainly with the eyes.

SKETCH OF A BALLET DANCER

Degas knew the rehearsal halls and backstage areas of the Opéra, the home of the ballet, but these places were often crowded, noisy and hectic. He preferred to draw the young dancers who became his subjects in his studio, where they could 'hold a pose' until he had committed to paper every detail he wanted.

TWO DANCERS

34

The diagonal pattern of white skirts and pink satin ballet shoes along the edge of the empty path of wood flooring leads to the benches on the back wall, where the dancers' mothers sit and wait. With fussy hats and wraps around their shoulders they silently encourage their daughters. Because ballet dancers almost always came from poor families, gaining a dancer's job on the Opéra stage was a way to a better life.

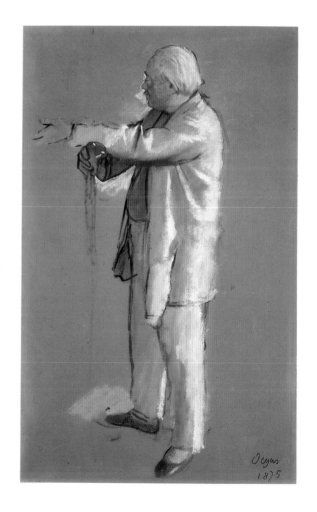

SEATED DANCER

RIGHT:
THE BALLET MASTER, JULES PERROT

Jules Perrot, once a great star of the ballet, was retired at the time this oil sketch was done. He did not mind posing while Degas captured the most characteristic details of his posture, dress and appearance, as well as patterns of light and shadow across his clothing. When Degas was ready to paint Perrot, he could do so without worrying that his model would get tired, for the sketch took the place of the man. In his painting, Degas changed little from the study: he put a white handkerchief in the old man's pocket and made his staff solid all the way to the floor. He also changed the gesture of Perrot's hand from one that questions to one that accepts.

Miss La La at the Cirque Fernando

Like many of his Parisian contemporaries, Degas was captivated by the daring acts of the circus. These were not travelling shows with big-top tents, but permanent theatres. The Cirque Fernando was the most famous in Paris, and Degas visited it often in January 1879 to make drawings of the acrobat Miss La La.

Degas must have recognized the practice and effort that went into Miss La La's sensational act. Holding on to a rope by the strength of her jaws, the young performer was hoisted high above the audience to the rafters of the circus pavilion. She moved her arms and legs in a hypnotic ballet as the hushed spectators craned their necks to follow her dangerous upward progress. Night after night, Degas drew her at the culmination of her act. Back in his studio, he produced this surprising painting.

Danger is suggested by the hot colour of the circus ceiling, which spills on to the arms and legs of the acrobat like the reflections of flames, and clashes with her own pink costume. Miss La La's off-centre position and Degas' viewpoint from below result in a dizzying imbalance. The angles of her arms, lower legs and feet echo those of the roof beams. The disorienting composition makes viewing the painting as tense and exciting an experience as being in the audience on the floor of the Cirque Fernando.

Degas' painting was carefully planned. After sketching Miss La La, he divided his drawing into squares. Next, he divided his canvas into the same number of squares, then he copied one square at a time from the sketch to the canvas.

Woman Ironing

Degas and his Opéra-going male friends all wore immaculate white, starched shirts, but they never saw them being laundered. Washing was done in

A WOMAN IRONING

places out of sight, in the basements of their homes or in the back rooms of laundry shops. However, writers of Degas' time wanted to explore themes of everyday urban life, and took an interest in the poor women of Paris who laundered shirts and did other menial tasks. These novelists may have inspired Degas to explore this new and unusual subject. In 1869, he drew a model posing as a laundry girl ironing, and in 1876, he took up the subject again. This time, he did not hire a model to act out the role. Instead, he went to a laundry shop.

It is likely that Degas made drawings in the company of laundry women for some time, for when he showed them to one of the great writers of his day — a man famous for his descriptions of the working men and women of Paris — the writer was amazed at their realism. Degas could even imitate the speech of the laundresses, and also knew the various strokes of the iron itself! He evidently had a gift for memorizing what he heard as well as what he saw.

Degas showed that ironing was hard work. The electric iron had not yet been invented; the iron that the laundress grasps in her right hand is made of heavy cast iron and was heated on top of a coal-fired stove. A wooden handle protected the laundress's hand from burns and made it easier to set a cool iron back on the stove and reach for a

hot one, for several were always waiting. A laundress had to perform this motion many times before a shirt was finished.

Degas' Starched Shirt

Degas arched the back of the laundress, splashed light across her shoulders, and made her right arm rigid to show that it takes hard work to make the iron glide. Reddened knuckles also show the harshness of her job. Her left hand deftly tugging wrinkles from the bright white shirt reveals her experience. A further testimony to her skill is the starched and folded shirt on her left.

With only one shirt done and many more drying on the lines across the windows, it must be the start of the day. Degas wanted to give the illusion of morning sun penetrating the half-wet shirts and illuminating the laundry room. To do this, he first painted the yellow-white curtains and the rose, ochre, lavender and blue shirts. He then scraped off the paint so that just coloured stains remained. He completed his painting by adding glazes, or layers of transparent colours, to show translucent cloth against light. His experiment worked. Sunshine floods into the room through layers of fabric. It illuminates the work-table, surrounds the laundress and silhouettes her face.

In an interesting contrast, Degas made the hanging laundry look more wearable than the starched, folded shirt on the table. Rolled cuffs, a stand-up collar, a slit for a front opening, and sharp, rectangular folds make it look as if it were carved out of marble instead of made of soft fabric. The starched shirt is totally rigid in a place where everything else is soft.

Stiffly starched shirts were the fashion for well-to-do men in Paris during Degas' time. This detail shows how Degas used a variety of colours to create a white shirt.

The Singer in Green

At night Degas found diversions from his art and, at the same time, sought new subjects for it. A host of noisy, flashy and crowded entertainment spots attracted him. They were the cafés-concerts, or 'caf'conç's' as they were familiarly called by the many people who enjoyed them.

Combining a bar where refreshments were cheap, a restaurant serving good food, and a stage for comic and sentimental entertainment, Paris's cafés-concerts had a loyal following. Degas frequented the more extravagant and expensive establishments, where famous singers were accompanied by full orchestras.

Drawing with Colour

Before electricity was widely used in theatres, performers were illuminated from below by the flames of burning gas jets that lined the front of the stage. Degas seemed to like the eerie effect of this flickering, unnatural light, so different from daylight coming from above. His young singer stands close to these harsh footlights, which throw shadows on her sloping shoulder and highlight her collarbone. Shadows also reach her face, circling her eyes. She is made to appear thinner and more fragile than she probably was. The unkind illumination robs her flesh of colour, but does not diminish the expressiveness of her black eyes. The bold gesture of her left hand contrasts strongly with the limp, uncertain attitude of her right hand.

Garish colours are made more strident by the flickering gaslights, and Degas seemed to delight in colouring the singer's skirt. Her golden-yellow bodice glows like brassy metal, and there is a similar intensity to the colour of the ribbons at her throat and in her hair. The palette of the gaudy costume served Degas for the background, too. The agitated marks of his pastels probably represent stage scenery or the outdoor garden of one of the cafés that Degas visited in summer.

By the time Degas made this drawing, he was working more often in pastels than in oil paints. Pastels gave Degas the opportunity to draw with pure colour. There was no waiting for them to dry, as with oils. Although they look like crayons, pastels contain no wax, and therefore have no sheen. Degas liked their matt finish. Today the term 'pastel colours' refers to soft and delicate hues, but Degas' pastels were strong and vibrant. They also gave him the freedom to scribble and smudge colours in the background.

In his letters, Degas mentioned particular singers with enthusiasm, commenting that one had 'the most spiritually tender voice imaginable'. He drew and painted a number of them.

The eager-to-please singer whom Degas drew with pastels seems young enough to be at the start of her career. Her face has not been identified as one of the known entertainers of the day, but she resembles a model Degas used for some dance subjects. The gesture of her left hand is also known; one of Degas' favourite singers used to tap her shoulder that way at the end of her songs to invite applause. It is possible that he combined drawings and mental pictures from various performances, while a model in his studio posed as the singer. Degas created an image of a girl leaving youthful innocence behind and awakening to her power over an audience.

The Millinery Shop

Perhaps it was the artificial nature of women's hats that inspired Degas to turn to these fashionable accessories of Parisian life as subject matter. According to one story, Degas was not daring enough to enter a millinery, or hat shop, on his own, so his friend Mary Cassatt, the American painter, let him accompany her. Many paintings of millinery shops followed.

Most millinery shops in nineteenth-century Paris were exclusive places selling to wealthy women. Hats were displayed on stands, arranged on a table covered in velvet. Except for the milliner and her colourful merchandise, this shop seems empty. The long sewing glove that extends up her right forearm and the pin between her pursed lips show that she

makes the hats she sells and is beginning to work on a new creation. Degas arranged her head and the table display so that a beautiful, ornate hat with hanging yellow-green ribbons is positioned like a colourful floral crown over her head.

The dark walls and curtains push the eyes forward to the brighter colours, keeping all the attention in the front. Hats punctuate the entire width of the painting. Degas obscured two hats in shadow. The other four hats are spotlighted and are brighter than their surroundings. The stands that support them blend with the shadows of the background and seem to disappear, making the hats appear to float. Out of an unremarkable scene of everyday life, Degas created a lively design.

Dancers, Pink and Green

Degas' famous ballet paintings reflect his enthusiasm for dance and how at home he was backstage at the Paris Opéra, the home of the ballet in Paris. He was equally familiar with the theatre's public boxes and stalls, from where he watched many performances. During his lifetime, he produced about fifteen hundred drawings, prints, pastels and oil paintings with ballet themes.

In *Dancers, Pink and Green*, each ballerina is caught in a characteristic pose as she waits to go on stage. One stretches and flexes her foot. Another secures her hair, while a third is almost hidden. The fourth dancer, who looks at her shoulder strap as she adjusts it, holds a pose that was a favourite of the artist and one he used in many paintings. An upright beam separates her from the fifth ballerina, who also turns her head but in the opposite direction, full of anticipation. Above her in the distance are the box seats, which Degas simplified into a stack of six red and orange rectangles along the edge of the canvas. The vertical beam the ballerina is touching extends to the top and the bottom of the painting. The multi-coloured vertical shapes behind the dancers represent a large, painted landscape used as a backdrop for one of the dances. It will provide a dream-world quality to the performance, as it does to the painting.

Imitation Charcoal Pencil Lines

Subscribers to the Opéra were allowed backstage in the theatre, and some took advantage of this access to pester dancers. On the far side of the tall wood column is the partial silhouette of a large man in a top hat. He seems to be trying to

Degas studied a subject long and hard before he painted it, but he also liked the Impressionist idea of capturing a fresh and vital impression. Here he brings the viewer backstage. The seemingly rapid and sketchy way of applying paint was another way of making the painting seem spontaneous.

keep out of the way, but his protruding profile overlaps a ballerina. None of the dancers pay attention to him. They also ignore one another, for this scene represents the tense moments just before the curtain rises.

Degas discovered that with oil paints he could achieve the same fresh feeling conveyed with pastels. Although this painting took the same amount of time to finish as many others and was designed and executed in his studio, Degas wanted to make it look as though it had been painted quickly, backstage. To do this, he imitated the marks of a charcoal pencil with his brush, making narrow black lines that edge the dancers' bodies and costumes. Next, he used his own innovation of simulating the matt finish of pastels by taking the sheen out of oil paint, then filling in the sketchy 'charcoal' outlines of his figures with a limited range of colours. The colours he used for the dancers extend to the floor and the background. The technique gives the impression that he applied the colours hastily while standing in the wings watching the dancers get ready.

The results of Degas' experiments could have been achieved much more quickly had he used pastels instead of oils. What Degas wanted, however, was to make paint look spontaneous. This was part of his lifelong quest: to make viewers feel that they were right there, beside him.

In spite of badly failing eyesight, Degas worked on for a dozen years after he finished *Dancers, Pink and Green*. It is hard to imagine the tragedy of a great painter going blind, but at the end of a brilliant career, it happened to Degas. Before his death in 1917, he spent ten years unable to see what he had painted.

As a young man, Degas wrote, 'In art you love and you produce only what you are used to.' He lived by those words, sharing his world with everyone who loved art.

When Degas was in his early twenties, and again some twenty years later, he copied the signatures of famous artists into his sketchbook. In the earlier version, he included his name, repeated in different styles as though the shaping of the letters might determine his success. His signature appears only once in the later book. It is written proudly and with confidence, the *s* identical to the *s* in Ingres' name. Degas had found his way without abandoning the lessons of his heroes. His career as an artist brought Old Master techniques and an Impressionist point of view into the twentieth century. If visions went through his mind after his sight had gone, one might have been of his famous signature alongside those of all the other immortals of art.

Late in his life, Degas made portraits of his family and friends using a camera instead of canvas and paint. He may have posed for himself to create this thoughtful and reflective portrait.

What Makes a Degas

The moments before or after an event interested Degas as much
as the event itself. He liked to portray scenes from contemporary life.

1.
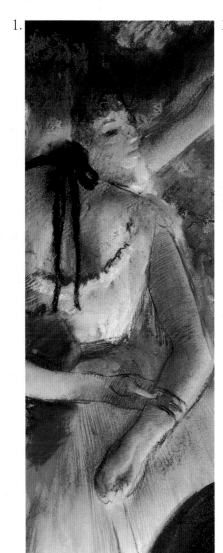

2.

3.

4.

1. Degas cut figures off at the edge
    of the canvas, creating a
    'snapshot' effect.

2. As if viewing it from above,
    Degas tipped the stage upward
    to prevent figures from blocking
    one another.

3. Degas used patches of brilliant
    colour to increase the feeling of
    movement.

4. Large, open spaces move the eye
    deep into the picture.

a Degas?

THE REHEARSAL OF THE BALLET ONSTAGE

Index